CATHOLIC
& MOURNING A LOSS

5 CHALLENGES AND 5 OPPORTUNITIES

MAURYEEN O'BRIEN, OP

acta
PUBLICATIONS

CATHOLIC & MOURNING A LOSS
5 CHALLENGES AND 5 OPPORTUNITIES
by Mauryeen O'Brien, OP

Edited by Gregory F. Augustine Pierce
Cover and text design and typesetting by Patricia A. Lynch
Cover photo courtesy of Bigstock

Scripture taken from *The Message*. Copyright © 1993, 1994, 1995, 1996, 2000, 2001, 2002. Used by permission of NavPress Publishing Group.

Copyright © 2014 by Maureen O'Brien

Published by ACTA Publications, 4848 N. Clark Street, Chicago, IL 60640, (800) 397-2282, www.actapublications.com

Library of Congress Catalogue Number: 2013955597
ISBN: 978-0-87946-524-7
Printed in the United States of America by United Graphics, Inc.
Year 25 24 23 22 21 20 19 18 17 16 15 14 13
Printing 20 19 18 17 16 15 14 13 12 11 10 9 8 7 6 5 4 3 2 First

CONTENTS

DEDICATION

To all who have reached out to those who mourn.
You are, indeed, among God's chosen ones.

INTRODUCTION

When we human beings have suffered a loss of any kind, we expect to go through a grieving process of some duration, depending on the nature and intensity of the event. It is part of our nature to mourn what we have loved.

Our grief may be caused by the death or sudden absence of a spouse, child, parent or sibling, friend, relative, or other loved one; or a colleague at work, companion in some activity, neighbor, member of a church or organization, or other acquaintance; or even a dog, cat, or other beloved pet. It could entail the loss of a job, home, financial security, health, youth, reputation, memory, lifelong dream, or prized possession. It could even be the loss of something or someone in the public arena that meant a lot to us.

Here is the reality: Unless we mourn that loss sufficiently and successfully, we will not be able to move on with our life and live it to its fullest. Our mourning can have no self-imposed time limit; it will not proceed logically or step by step; and it may surround us over and over again. There is no way around our grief. We cannot go over it or under it or around it; we must work *through* it, and that may be the hardest work we ever attempt.

What can help us navigate our grief journey? There are innumerable therapists, support groups, books, movies, music and lectures available. There are experienced church personnel, family, and friends who are willing to listen to and support us as we try to make some sense of what has happened. We should make use of as many of these resources as are helpful.

But we may ask ourselves: "Where is God in what I am going through?" We may temporarily lose our sense of God's presence in the throes of our grief: "Why does God allow such pain and suffering?" These are questions for which we try to find answers over and over again throughout our life. We may even find it difficult at times to pray; it may seem we are only able to cry and be angry and be in pain. Trusting in God's power and ability to intervene in our life may be a very difficult thing for us to do at these times.

However, precisely *because* our loss, no matter what its nature, is forcing us to assess our spiritual life, the act of struggling with our grief can actually help us experience the presence of a loving God in an even stronger way. And our Catholic faith, with its strong emphasis on forgiveness and healing and prayer, can help that happen.

We Catholics believe Jesus taught us that God, whom he experienced as a loving Father, wants only good things for us. We believe Jesus showed us by his own example how to accept and overcome sorrow and loss, even the most unjust. And we believe Jesus never judges or abandons us as we struggle with our grief.

Catholic prayer and ritual can therefore be an important element of the healing process. They provide a framework of faith for us to overcome our sadness and anger through the use of repetition and familiarity. They allow us to express our deepest thoughts and feelings about loss and death. In times of grief they can bring us a sense of balance and peace. They give us a way to say goodbye, to express our pain, to adjust to transitions, to remember treasured times and people and things that have brought beauty and meaning to our life. They help connect us with our past, define our present, and show us a path to the future.

Certainly we all need to rely on faith and trust in God if we are to embrace the healing that can take place after experiencing a loss of any kind. Our Catholic faith prompts us to understand that life is not just happy or just sad; it is a combination of the two. Our faith can help us begin to realize that even though loss always produces suffering and pain, we can recover from it and move on with life. We need only look at the happenings in Christ's life here on earth from Good Friday to Easter Sunday to realize that out of suffering can come great joy and the promise of new life.

Mourning a loss has its challenges. When we grieve we become extremely vulnerable. We stand with open, raw wounds in need of healing and compassion. We wonder if we are strong enough to meet the tasks before us. "How can I ever heal?" we may say. "How can I begin to live a new life when the life I have been living, which was so happy and full, has been lost forever?"

Catholic prayer and ritual can bring us a sense of balance and peace, a way to remember people who have brought beauty and meaning to our life.

In my work over decades with people like you, dear reader, who have suffered a loss, I have found that facing head-on the challenges of mourning is really the only way to move successfully through the grieving process. You will be challenged; there is no doubt about that. But with each challenge there will arise an opportunity to grow stronger as you struggle to face the changes that inevitably come because of every sorrow you endure.

FIRST CHALLENGE

Our ability to work through the grieving process will be tested.

Someone once said that the work of grieving is the hardest work we ever do. There are many things we have to face when we have lost someone or something that enriched our life—emotions we must look at, some we might never have experienced before.

Madeline, a seventy-four-year-old lady I work with as a grief counselor, confided to me that she had never really been an angry person. She found little to be angry about—until, that is, her landlord told her she had to get rid of her dog because it barked too much and disturbed the neighbors.

"I found myself furious with him," she told me. "How dare he try to take away my Toby when he was all I had left after my husband died?" Her realization that she could get so angry was new for her, and she didn't like the feeling. She and I discussed at length that the loss of her dog was part of her grieving the death of her husband and that it added to her feeling of abandonment. "I'm not sure I can work through this grieving process," she said. "It's too hard, and I'm not strong enough to handle it anymore."

My friend was questioning her ability to be able to face

the sense of sorrow and loss she was going through. It was hard work, and she was tired and sad and lonely.

"I was downsized last month in a job I had held for fifteen years," a man named Jack said to me one day. "I loved my job and did it well. I even received commendations from my supervisor. People often remarked that the company would never have grown as it did if it wasn't for me and the work that I did. And then, out of the blue, I was let go! Now, I don't know what to do. That job was my whole life. I almost feel there is nothing to live for, nowhere to go. I know I have to mourn the loss of my job, but I can't face working through the whole grief thing."

Madeline and Jack are both going through losses they need to work through but feel they don't have the strength or even the ability to do so. They are tired, discouraged, questioning, and confused. Madeline feels there is now absolutely no one there for her. Jack, who worked so hard to gain an important role in his company, feels that he is no longer useful. Both are mourning their loss but lack the strength to face their grief.

There may be times we find ourselves unable to understand the losses we have gone through. We may consider them just part of life or decide to try and forget them or put them aside until we get the time to really think about them. In the meantime, we may be feeling the effects of not facing the grief these losses have caused.

There may be times we find ourselves unable to understand our losses.

Here are some ideas to think about as we question our ability to face our grief and try to find the strength to work through it:

■ **Because grief-work is so difficult, we need to be prepared physically as well as emotionally to face what will be demanded of us.** We must take the time to eat properly, to rest when we are tired, to see a doctor if we are feeling sick. This is a time when we need to pamper ourselves a bit. If we feel like doing something, we need to do it! If something we want to avoid can wait until tomorrow, we need to let it wait! We mustn't push ourselves to overdo when we are grieving. Let those who offer to do something physical for us (like, go grocery shopping or mow our lawn or give us a massage) be of help. We need to acknowledge the fact that a rested, healthy body is important as we tackle the hard work of moving through our grief.

■ **We should pay attention to our emotions.** Grief can give rise to feelings that we may never even realize we have. We can come to terms with those emotions by talking about them to a trusted friend or counselor. Our emotions are neither good nor bad; they are just how we feel. It's what we do with those emotions and how we express them that really matters. Loss and the change it brings can cause our emotions to fluctuate over and over again. Unless they are acknowledged and worked with, they can hinder our moving through the grieving process.

- **We cannot ever compare ourselves to others who are grieving.** Everyone lives and loves differently from those around them. So, too, will we all mourn differently. Two people may lose their jobs on the same day, even in the same company, for example, but each may react differently—even oppositely—to their loss. Neither will do it "perfectly," because there is no perfect way to grieve. The only thing that will be the same is the knowledge that they will have to persevere through the grief process if they are to face the possibility of a new life after their loss.

- **We have to avoid looking for strength in things that can harm us.** Alcohol, drugs, junk food, even smoking may give us relief for a time, but that is only temporary and may become addictive. We need to use this time to turn to God, who knows us intimately and has promised to be there for us. In this we can lean heavily on our Catholic faith, which can sustain us, and its sacraments, which can nourish us, and its prayers and rituals, which can lift us up. Let us follow the Jesus of the New Testament. His life on earth was filled with sorrow and loss: father, friends, followers, perhaps

even his hopes and dreams. He knew what it is to experience pain and suffering. Yet he held out to all of
us, even at the moment of his deepest anguish, the
promise of new life.

FIRST OPPORTUNITY

We can learn to use the gifts that working through grief has offered us.

A man named Phil called me one day to ask for help. "Church help," he explained, and then he proceeded to tell me his story. His wife of twelve years had just left him and his four children—ages two, four, six, and eight—and he was devastated. "I can't even get out of bed in the mornings," he said. "How am I going to be able to take care of my kids, much less myself?"

Phil soon learned that he needed to help himself first, before he could be there for his children. At my urging he joined a Catholic support group that helped him face and then work through the sadness and sense of loss caused by his failed relationship with his wife. "It was probably the best thing I have ever done for myself," he told me later. "That group reached out to me and showed me that God was walking with me every step of my journey, no matter how painful it was."

"And not only that," he continued, "I soon began to realize that God was giving me the ability to stand up again for myself and my kids, with his help, of course."

To Phil, being able to turn to God and receive the ability to "stand up again" was a great gift. He had come to the group beaten down, confused, discouraged, filled with pain and suffering. He thought he was a weak man, not realizing that all his emotional strength had been zapped out of him. Once he realized that turning to God could give him great strength, he was able to do what he (and his children) needed him to do. "I never thought that out of all this mess I could become strong again," he said. "What a gift!"

Let's look at some of the gifts we can receive as we work through mourning various losses—some big, some small:

- **Finding new meaning in and appreciation of life.** I am now in my sixties. So many of us dread "old age" and the diminished capacities it often brings. Many times our health deteriorates, friends and family pass away, the ability to take part in activities or late-night get-togethers fades. Simple tasks become challenges that many times seem beyond endurance. But we older folk use our extended age as a true gift. Our wisdom has been tested and tried, and we find we are no longer afraid to share it with others. Our experience far surpasses that of the young, our capacity to love and to forgive has widened and stretched, and we have learned to share these insights and lessons with the next generation and even the generation after that!

- **Encountering the love of God in a new and real way.** When those of us who mourn feel we have lost "everything," when we feel completely empty and alone, we often seem to be "pushed" or even "forced" to turn to God, and there we discover a power that loves us—one we were often not able to feel before our loss. It's almost as if our emptiness becomes a gift, for we finally realize that only God can fill the void and only our faith can sustain us. As painful as learning that lesson is, we recognize it as a blessing.

■ **Opening up and sharing.** One of the best things we learn to do for ourselves as we work through the grieving process is to share our thoughts and feelings with others, especially those who have gone through a similar loss. No longer do we have to bury our grief if we can learn to speak about it. A wise poet once said, "…grief shared is grief diminished." For in sharing our pain and suffering we are able to learn from one another. Understanding, compassion, and wisdom are many times born within a community or with friends who are open to grieving together the losses we are going through.

 **Emptiness can become a gift when we realize that only God can fill the void.**

■ **Saying final goodbyes.** There is holiness to saying goodbye to a loved one, a pet, or even a beloved thing or life situation. These have been with us throughout our life, and now we get to appreciate just how much they have meant to us. We are allowed to "let them go" while still loving them. Of course we mourn the fact that we cannot see or hear or touch them again, yet we long for a way to feel their presence. Our Catholic faith tells us that there is more to life than what we see, and we come to believe this in a very deep and real way.

■ **Treasuring our memories.** Another gift that comes from grief is a new-found ability to remember. We know we need to find a new place in our emotions for our lost loved ones. They can no longer be physically present to us, but they can become emotionally and spiritually present. In order for that to happen, we must begin to create "cherishable memories" of them by actively reviving and reviewing the stories of our relationship with them. The remembering and the telling of those stories can be transformed into images capable of becoming part of our very being. There will certainly be tears—lots of them—as we remember, but eventually they will transform into tears of joy. We will come to realize that the images of our beloved people, animals, and things will never desert us if we can hold on to our memory of them.

SECOND CHALLENGE

Our life will be changed because of our loss.

Loss forever changes the world of the bereaved. Something or someone or some situation that has enriched our life is no longer there. We find ourselves in a new environment, personally and socially. An ending to what was so familiar and comfortable to us has occurred, and we hesitate to face a new beginning. We ask ourselves if we are strong enough to adjust to yet another change in our life, perhaps the most difficult one we have been asked to endure, one we hoped would never occur. We probably had become comfortable with doing things the way we always had, and now with this particular loss we realize that life may become quite uncomfortable and unhappy for a considerable time. Or we may think our sorrow will simply never abate, much less end.

I had been seeing Bill for a number of weeks after he lost his job as one of the vice-presidents of a large company. I knew he wasn't working during the time he was seeing me, and so I wondered why he appeared at my office each time all dressed up in business suit and tie and always with a briefcase. I asked him why he presented himself as if he were going to work, even though both of us knew he wasn't. "I can't face the fact that I don't have a job anymore," he said. "I find it hard each morning when I get up to admit my whole world has changed. I loved my job; I looked forward to going to work; I felt what I did was very important. Now I think that if I just keep dressing the part, someone will want to hire me. I just can't face give up putting on my work clothes each day, because then I would have to begin to deal with what I have lost and may never find again."

Bill's world had certainly changed. He had lost something that seemed to define his role in the world, something that he enjoyed and even loved, and he had turned to pretending he was still employed in order not to face the pain that his loss was demanding of him. How difficult it was for him to accept this particular change in his life!

"I can't believe how my whole life has changed since my husband died," a widow named Catherine said to me one day. "I never noticed before, but everyone seems to do things in pairs. For example, John and I belonged to a bridge club that met every Friday night. Since I've lost him as my partner, I feel I've also lost the others in the club. I feel I will never see them again, yet I don't want to go and play with another partner." Catherine also told me that she had decided not to attend her nephew's wedding the following month. "Whom would I sit with, or who would be there to dance with me?" she asked.

Catherine's life had suddenly changed with the death of her husband. She was no longer a "couple" in her world that was filled with couples. Her solution was to run away and not to take part anymore in the social things that once gave her such joy, even though intellectually she understood that was not a viable plan if she was ever going to be happy again.

Here are some challenges we might face due to a loss:

- **The loss of companionship.** Whether it is because of the death of a loved one or a beloved pet, a divorce or separation, a child going off to college or getting his or her own apartment, a retirement or loss or change of job, a move to a new neighborhood or even city, or some other change in our daily routine, we can lose contact with people we love or at least are used to interacting with. We have to make an effort to keep in touch with them if we can and build new relationships if needed. For example, I encouraged Catherine to start out with simple things, like calling a close relative to go with her to her nephew's wedding. She also started to attend the bridge club as a substitute when one of the members couldn't attend. Eventually she found another person whose partner had moved out of town, and they began playing regularly together.

- **The loss of meaning and purpose.** Any kind of loss can tempt us to throw up our hands and say, "What's the use of living?" What we are really saying is "What's the use of continuing my life if it has lost meaning and purpose?" The fact is that we get to assign or identify the meaning and purpose of our lives. As Catholics, we start with the fact that we are a son or daughter of God and build from there.

- **The loss of self-esteem and identity.** Bill felt that if he did not have a job he did not have an identity. While it is true that his identity may have changed from "Bill who does this for a living," to "Bill who is looking for a new job but is a great guy with lots going for him." The challenge is to recognize that our self-esteem comes from within, not from how others perceive us.

- **The loss of faith.** Why do bad things happen to good people? Rabbi Harold Kushner famously asked this question over thirty years ago. This is what most of us ask when something bad happens to us or to a loved one. It is the ultimate religious question, because it goes to our belief in the very nature of a good God. And the answer is not simple or obvious or easy to ascertain. Our Catholic faith has been struggling with this since the crucifixion of Jesus of Nazareth, and we continue to ask it today. Some people lose their faith—at least for a time—when they suffer a devastating loss. Others find great comfort in it. And most of us struggle with it. It is, in many cases, one of the main challenges in the mourning process.

 **The challenge is to recognize that our self-esteem comes from within.**

SECOND OPPORTUNITY

We can realize that change can be an opportunity for newness and growth.

There are very few of us who actually embrace any kind of change in our lives. There seems to be security in things that are stable and structured. We may not even enjoy some of what we cling to, but at least we know what they entail because we have done them or lived with them for years. Mourning a loss offers the opportunity to look again at our lives, to reconsider the realities—the "new normal" as they call it in grief literature—and to grow by seeking and adopting different ways of thinking, acting, and believing.

When things are always the same, day after day, our life can become stagnant and hum-drum. It's easy to stay with the familiar, but is it productive, challenging or even healthy for us? We all need the opportunity for newness in our lives. The world is filled with wonderful surprises that can enhance and enrich us. Sure, we'd all like change to come without any sorrow or pain, but that is not the way of the physical world. There will be losses—some big, some small—and these losses will challenge us with the changes they force upon us. But there is also an opportunity they present, if we are willing to grasp it.

Change can bring suffering, but it can also bring growth. The challenges that we encounter when we mourn can open both our heart and our mind to "try on" a world we might never have known existed. That newness can call forth ideas and feelings we may never have had the opportunity to voice or live before.

Mary loved living in the town in which she grew up. Everything and everyone was familiar to her. Being able to go into a store or eat at one of the many restaurants in town and be known by name gave her a sense of well-being and security. When Tom asked her to marry him, the one little stipulation she made was that they remain in her hometown during their married life. Tom went along with it because he knew how happy it made Mary. Besides, he liked the town and soon became as much a part of it as Mary had always been.

About three years into their marriage, however, Tom was offered a big promotion in his job that would entail moving to a city clear across the country. When he approached Mary with the idea of moving, she melted into tears. "You promised me we could stay here," she said. "I wouldn't know what to do in a place where no one knows me or the surroundings aren't familiar."

Both Tom and Mary came to me to talk about their dilemma. Tom was excited about being picked for this promotion and visualized all they could do with the money they would receive with his salary increase. He was anxious to try something new and felt that this job would give him the opportunity to be creative and make a big contribution to the company that had put its trust in his capabilities.

Mary, on the other hand, was scared of the new. She really had surrounded herself with the familiar and felt she could not give up the security it afforded her. The thought of change seemed very threatening to her.

These two people were still very much in love, and each of them saw the other person's point. Eventually they worked out an agreement where they made the move for Tom's job but built into their new, improved family budget many trips every year back to Mary's home town and an intention to retire there at the end of Tom's career. It wasn't a perfect solution, but it has worked so far, partly because both of them understand the other's needs and make a real effort to make the "new normal" succeed.

Here are a few ideas we talked about when I met with Mary and Tom. They seemed to help them; maybe they can help the rest of us as we face any sort of loss.

- **We all need to face the fact head-on that the loss we have to accept will bring a change in our life.** Life itself is not static: it is ever-changing. Change brings with it the possibility of growth and newness. We can embrace the change without abandoning our feelings for what we have lost.

- **We must adapt and ask for help to those changes that occur in our life because of loss.** For example, if we have lost a spouse or life companion, we shouldn't allow ourselves to be caught, especially in a social situation, where we will feel awkward and alone. You know all those friends who are always asking if there is anything they can do to help? Say yes! They will be delighted. Ask them to accompany you when you need someone to go somewhere with you, whether it is a family event, a church fund-raiser, or just a visit to Starbucks or a walk around the block. You will be surprised how willing (and pleased) people will be to respond.

■ **We cannot allow ourselves to wallow in self-pity or cut ourselves off from others.** At a time of mourning, more than at any other times, we need to surround ourselves with those who love us—accept their invitations; call them up; make or renew some friendships. If you are shy or don't have a lot of friends, get more active in your church. It is full of people just like you, many mourning losses of their own.

■ **We should be open to the "new" in our life.** The past may have been filled with joy and happiness, things that we can cherish forever. But the future can bring with it many surprises that can nourish us as well as we begin to move through and beyond our days of mourning. We can take a class, start or go back to a hobby, volunteer to help those less fortunate than we are (and there is always someone less fortunate than we are).

■ **As Catholics, we must rely strongly on the God who loves us and knows what we need and never fails to give it.** We can seek him at Mass, in daily prayer and meditation, on a retreat, or in service to others. We need to take some quiet moments in the course of each day to share our fears and anxieties with our friend and brother, Jesus. If we have a special devotion to his mother, Mary, or one of the saints, now is the time to call on their intercession. If there is a prayer or grief group in our parish, we should overcome our reluctance and join it. Praying and talking with others can give us a renewed sense of companionship and a feeling of belonging.

- **As Catholics, we also can look to the life that Jesus modeled for us when he was on earth.** No day seemed to be the same for Jesus. He left the security of his home in Nazareth to face a world that could not accept the changes he opened to them. His own people expected to be saved by a King, but Jesus came to them as a poor, itinerant preacher. His was a call for change; an opportunity for his followers to embrace the new and to grow. Some accepted Jesus' offer; many didn't. But he clearly came to bring change to a world that was filled with sorrow and pain. He embraced change; he preached change; he lived change. And he changed the world!

- **We must never hesitate to ask God in prayer to help us face the changes that are inevitable in our life.**

 **Praying and talking with others can give us a renewed sense of companionship.**

We must take the chance that if God asks us to be open to the opportunities for growth that he places before us, he will be there to walk beside us as you work through them.

- **Finally, we can be aware of the many new people we may meet as a result of a change in our life.** New people may open us to new ideas, information, and supportive friendships. Each one of them can be helpful in allowing us to grow into a more knowledgeable, sensitive and compassionate person. (For example, Marie's new best friend, Eileen, is a woman Marie met in the new city she and Tom moved to. She would never have met Eileen had she not been open to the move.)

THIRD CHALLENGE

Our ability to function will be questioned.

When we go through loss, especially a "big" one (that is, big to us), our whole world can seem to turn upside down. We can become confused, unable to understand what is happening to us, not really accepting the loss, somehow convincing ourselves our loss never happened or hasn't really affected us. Sometimes we don't seem to be able to make decisions on our own, and many times we simply don't make them at all. We become depressed and disoriented, waiting for what we have loved and lost to come back into our lives.

I worked with a young woman named Annie a number of years ago after she arrived at my office a month after her husband had died. She told me she needed to tell me what she had been going through during that month.

"For the first twenty-nine days since my husband, Don, died," she said, "I found myself at five o'clock each evening sitting in the living room waiting for him to unlock the front door and come in after work. Finally, on the thirtieth day, I finally realized he would never again be unlocking that front door. I had been waiting for something I knew intellectually couldn't possibly happen, and yet emotionally I wasn't able to accept that."

Annie was certainly in a state of denial that left her helpless and confused. She kept saying to me, "I can't function on my own. I need Don to be there for me. I'll never get through the rest of my life without him."

Annie certainly was questioning her ability to function on her own. When Don was around, she had thought of herself as a strong, independent, self-sufficient woman. Decisions came easy for her when she had Don to consult. He was strong when the difficult things came along. She knew she could always rely on him to talk things over and explore all sides of a question with her before she had to decide something. This had become a pleasant way of life for her. Now she felt that every decision, every hardship, every move she made would have to be faced alone. She feared she wouldn't have the strength or even the ability to do that, yet she didn't want to become dependent on others to help her.

At the other end of the spectrum was Allen, a man I counseled who had lost his once-prized and deep relationship with his wife when she asked him for a divorce. "I've found someone else who really understands me," she told him.

"The irony was that I had struggled for years to understand her, and it all went down the drain with that one statement," he told me. "I'm giving up on other people," he said. "As long as I can remain completely independent, the better off I'll be. I'm the only one I can really count on!"

Annie and Allen, both grieving a similar loss, turned in on themselves for comfort and consolation, but in opposite ways. Annie lost her confidence in herself; Allen lost his trust in anyone else. What they share is that they are both afraid they will lose their ability to function independently. By refusing help from others—either because they can't or won't ask—each of them ends up questioning (and having others question) his or her ability to care for themselves and others.

Here are a few things for us to consider as we face the challenge of functioning on our own after a loss:

- **We must recognize that to be independent doesn't mean to remain alone.** We need the input of others as we make big decisions in our life. None of us have all the answers. That's a part of the human condition, but getting the input of others can help us look at the whole picture rather than just one part of it. (Annie was right about what Don had provided for her; now she needed to find someone else to take his place in that regard. It could be her parents, or a best friend, or even a paid counselor. But if she was to be truly independent she needed others to rely on. This is the real paradox of mourning a loss.)

- **We cannot be stoic in the face of loss.** We can neither "tough it out" nor "go it alone." We have to share with others, especially our family and friends, the sorrow that is in our heart. This doesn't make us dependent; it gives us the opportunity to grieve, and that can't always be done alone. In fact, it almost never can be done alone. (In this respect, Allen was totally on the wrong path, which I was able to convince him of after provided a lot of time and talking.)

■ We have to seek advice from those who have gone through what we are experiencing now. We can't be afraid to talk to people who have also lost something similar to what we have lost. They certainly have learned something from their journey through grief. Let them walk with us on our difficult journey. That is why so many people find grief support groups valuable—they are a "safe" place where people can share what they have gone and are going through.

■ **We must ask God for help.** Prayer may not come too easily at this time, so we shouldn't feel we have to say all those formal prayers we may have learned as a child. A simple, "Jesus, help me," can call forth a God who loves you and has promised to be there for you.

■ **We can read and reflect.** There are many books dealing with grief that are available to us. People will inundate us with them! We have to take them slowly, think about what we are reading, and share with someone the questions they may evoke. Perhaps we can keep a journal of our feelings after reading and reflecting and return to that journal often as we try to sort out our feelings. A second and third reading of something that really touches us can often give us many new insights.

THIRD OPPORTUNITY

We can explore the new-found strength that can be ours.

Betty had always hosted the Thanksgiving dinner for her extended family. It had become a large, formal event that everyone seemed to look forward to. "I even send out invitations," she told me, "with a P.S. asking that they bring certain special items for the dinner, and they always do. But I'm not sure I can do it this year."

She explained that her husband, Fred, had died only two months earlier and she was afraid there would be a sadness around the Thanksgiving table on her behalf. "I imagine no one will want to even mention his name for fear I will melt into tears," she said. "Yet I want so much to hear his name and remember him with my family, even though I may well cry. I keep wondering if I should really host Thanksgiving this year, so soon after his death."

We talked together about Betty's hesitation, and both of us promised we would pray that she make the right decision. A few days after Thanksgiving, Betty called to tell me what she had decided and what had happened. She held the dinner, and those who attended heeded the invitation to bring their usual mashed potatoes or gravy or string bean salad or dessert. And her family also responded to a second P.S. she had placed in each invitation. It read: "You may not attend Thanksgiving dinner this year unless you bring with you a funny story about Fred that you will share with those around the table."

She told me that her table rocked with laughter, that she became aware of things about Fred she had never known. She heard her husband's name over and over again, and that was a real blessing to her. "I not only felt wonderful," she said, "I felt stronger than I had ever been since Fred's death." "It's strange," she confided, "I never thought I would laugh again, and here I was eager to share the joy that Fred obviously brought to so many people. With every story and every laugh, I seemed to grow stronger and stronger."

Betty's decision to invite others to be there for her during her time of her grieving was a choice she made completely on her own (perhaps with a little help from the Almighty). The idea that she could make that choice gave her a feeling of independence that led to a strength she hadn't realized she possessed.

Let's look at some ways we might explore our new-found strength in the midst of our grieving:

- **We can start to develop new skills.** For example, perhaps your deceased husband was a good plumber or electrician around the house. Or perhaps your deceased wife was a good cook or homemaker. Or perhaps your deceased child ran errands for you or helped you with the computer. Now that your loved one is no longer with you, those roles still need to be performed. You will have to decide whether you should learn to do them yourself or get someone else to do so. In either case, you will be in charge. If you do begin to learn new skills, you will find a new inner strength and a feeling of accomplishment. And wouldn't your loved one be proud of you!

■ **We shouldn't be afraid to take "baby steps."** The journey through grief is a long, difficult one. Many times we can put off beginning that journey because it seems impossible to face the stumbling blocks along the way. We have to convince ourselves that we can take one step at a time and must take all the time we need to go from one step to another.

■ **We have to reach out to those who have offered their help.** Struggles can become easier if we share them with others. If we refuse the help of others, we not only miss the opportunity to learn from them and experience their care and concern but also worry them about our own stability and competence. They know, at least instinctively, that they are an important source of strength that we desperately need, and if we reject their help it is a sign that we are *not* doing as well as we claim.

 **We must take all the time we need to go from one "baby step" to another.**

■ **As Catholics, we should not hesitate to call on God.** We have learned from childhood that God is there for us when we are in any kind of need. Our suffering from a particular loss may be too much for us to handle at the moment, so we need to ask God to handle it for us. The author of the prayer/poem, "Footprints," sums it up God's answer in these words: "My precious child, I love you and I would never leave you. During your times of trial and suffering, when you see only one set of prints, it was then I carried you."

■ **We can share our memories.** Every time we recount a memory, we build up within ourselves images that become part of us. This helps us form a new relationship with that which we have lost. The more "cherished memories" we collect and share, the stronger our inner attachment can become. Although a physical presence is no longer there, a spiritual and emotional presence can be attained.

FOURTH CHALLENGE

Our dreams for the future may have to be altered.

Loss, no matter what kind, usually brings about change, and so we may find ourselves unable to even think about the future. The present, with its day-to-day difficulties, seems hard enough to live through, so we may have the tendency to put our dreams for the future aside. This eventually can compound our initial loss, however. There is a strength and a hope in following a dream, and to surrender our dreams may leave us weak and vulnerable. It certainly can cause us to be sad and depressed.

Nate, a young man of twenty-six, stopped in my office one day to talk about what was going on in his life. He had been studying at medical school for the past two years when suddenly he came down with a rare disease that left him very weak, especially in his arms and hands. "There is no cure for it," he told me. "I'll be this way the rest of my life. There goes my dream of being a doctor."

Naturally, Nate was discouraged; who wouldn't be? He had studied hard, worked many part-time jobs, and saved his money, all in preparation to begin his medical career. He had wanted to be a doctor since he was eight years old; now that reality would never be achieved. "I dreamed the dream," he said. "And now I've lost that dream forever."

"What's the sense of fashioning a dream?" a young woman named Elena confided to me one day after she had failed the entrance test to law school. "Somehow, it never gets fulfilled. Either you don't have the money or the education or the support to move beyond the ordinary, and so it doesn't take much to give up that dream. So why dream at all?"

Both of these young people began their quests at a young age, both looked forward to fulfilling them, and both were now facing the hardships and challenges they would encounter because of their seemingly lost dreams.

"Would it have been better if I hadn't planned for my future at all?" Nate asked me. "It seems to me I would have saved myself a lot of disappointment and sadness."

I knew Nate well enough to realize that if he hadn't followed his dream, he would have faced even more disappointment. Nate's heart was big, full of love and desire to help others. Being a doctor could be a wonderful way to accomplish that. Now that the door was closed to that, he would have to find another dream that would allow him to reach out to those who needed his help.

"I guess I'm just not smart enough to be a lawyer," Elena said. "Maybe I'm not smart enough to do anything worthwhile."

My prayer for both of these young people was that they would come to the realization that one of the challenges of mourning a loss is to search out other dreams that open us to new worlds and bring us new happiness and fulfillment.

Here are some ideas that may help us continue to dream despite the losses we encounter:

- **We can't give up!** Unless we set goals for ourselves after a loss, we may get stuck in the process of mourning. Every one of us needs to be able to look forward to something, to be challenged to go beyond what we think we can do, despite our sorrow.

- **If we determine one dream is no longer attainable, we have to go for another.** The mind and the heart are made to expand, to look toward horizons where the sun is rising, not setting. There is always a world of possibilities waiting for us to explore. (Nate finally came to realize this and pursued a career in medical research. Elena never got over her rejection to law school and never replaced that dream with another.)

- **We can't just wish we could have a new dream.** We have to prepare ourselves to pursue it. It may take more education, different experiences, more money,

 **New dreams can open us to new worlds and bring us new happiness and fulfillment.**

and wiser decisions on our part. But the payoff will be well worth it.

- **We shouldn't be afraid to ask for help.** Many times dreams can be realized if we are humble enough to ask those around us who have also followed their dream. They will lend us an ear and share some advice. There is nothing like the experience of others to give us the strength to continue a journey that is sometimes very difficult. And remember, almost everyone who has pursued a dream have experienced hardships, loss, and challenges that got in their way and had to be overcome.

- **First, of course, we must acknowledge that we are mourning the loss of a past dream.** We have to grieve that loss, examine what it meant to us, and accept the fact that our life will (and should) go on in spite of it. Only then can we be open to the possibility of a new life with a new dream.

- **Who more than Jesus would understand what the loss of a dream is all about?** His dreams were shattered many times during his short life here on earth. And yet, discouraged as he might have been, he endured all sorts of hardships and disappointments in order to continue to dream about "a new heaven and a new earth," as it says in the Book of Revelation.

FOURTH OPPORTUNITY

We can go beyond ourselves as we face the future.

It's a wonderful thing to seek what seems to be impossible. It stretches us, opens doors that have appeared closed, and expands horizons we've never dreamed were accessible to us.

Shirona had been an average student in high school. Her math grades pulled her average down and she found herself at graduation time toward the bottom of her class. She decided she had had enough of school and didn't apply to college, as most of her classmates had.

"It was time for me to get a job," she told me. "I knew I could make some money and really enjoy life."

Well, Shirona got a job, but, of course, it was at the entry level, and the money she made was barely enough to get her from one paycheck to the next.

"I kept applying for advancement," she told me, "but each time I did, I was told I needed to further my education in order to be considered for a new position."

Finally, Shirona came to the realization that if she were to get anywhere in life, she would have to put aside the disappointments she encountered in high school and open herself to a new educational experience in college.

"I don't know if I can do it," she said one day. "I wasted so much time in high school that I don't think I have the background to even attempt college."

Shirona didn't realize it, but she gave me the word I needed to try to convince her that she was bright enough to follow a college career.

"Shirona," I said, "you used the word 'attempt' when you were talking to me about going to college. That's all I ask you to do: attempt college."

That must have rung a bell for her. She enrolled in college in the fall of the year that we talked together. It was a struggle for her, but struggle she did! And with each challenge she encountered, each obstacle she met, she fought hard and persevered.

I saw Shirona a few years after she graduated. What a change I saw in her. She had found a strength and determination in the midst of the hardships and expectations of college life. She was no longer content to just "be." She had learned to go beyond that, and in so doing, had prepared herself for new and exciting possibilities. She was no longer satisfied with the "entry level" position. She now had new skills, more confidence, and the expectation she could at least "attempt" what she had thought was the impossible.

Here are a few things we might try in order to open ourselves to new possibilities that could enhance our future after a loss:

- **We can apply ourselves to every opportunity that comes our way.** We can seek the new, not be content with what is. We were created to grow emotionally, intellectually, and spiritually. That certainly is a challenge, but the end results can be extremely fulfilling. (Shirona now has a well-paying job with benefits that she loves.)

- W**e have to surround ourselves with positive people and learn as much as we can from them.** What has made them so positive? What were some of the obstacles they had to overcome? Were they always positive about life or did they have to stretch themselves in order to become so?

- **We can't be afraid to accept a challenge.** It may be easier to remain safe and comfortable after a loss, but we'll never grow that way. Each challenge, though it may demand hard work and the possibility of change, can give us the opportunity to go beyond ourselves as we face the future.

 **It may be easier to remain safe and comfortable after a loss, but we'll never grow that way.**

- **We have to find ways to nourish our prayer life.** First step is to find a comfortable way to speak to God. Is it through reflection, meditation, centering prayer, just plain talking or listening? We should try whatever methods open our heart and soul to God's loving presence. The trick is to pray often, listen attentively, and love with an open heart.

- **We must have confidence in God and in ourselves.** We have most certainly been given the gifts necessary to live a good and productive life, even after an important loss. There may be challenges along the way (you can be sure of that!), but God will never ask us to go it alone. We mustn't be afraid to ask, and keep on asking God to walk with us as we journey beyond our grief in order to face the future more productively and peacefully.

FIFTH CHALLENGE

We will question our reliance on others and even on God.

How many times in our life have we Catholics heard that if we ask God for anything, it will be given to us; if we pray hard enough, our prayers will be answered? The answer is probably hundreds of times: ever since childhood, whenever there is a problem, when we go to church and listen to homilies. And yet, how many times when things didn't go as we wanted, did we question whether or not God was even listening to us, or maybe even there?

Jose, a hard-working carpenter who had just been laid off from his job, asked that question of me when we met a few months ago.

"Where is God in my life right now?" he said. "I could sense that a number of us were going to be laid off at work, and so I did a lot of praying. And I asked everyone I met to do the same thing. But despite all those prayers, I'm now without a job! Why hasn't God heard me?"

Jose was angry, discouraged and very confused. He was experiencing the loss of his job and anticipating all the hardships that would follow.

"I won't even have the money to pay my mortgage next

month," he said. "And then, besides losing my job, I'll lose my home. And God doesn't even care."

Jose needed to vent, and he needed to mourn the loss of his job and maybe his home. Going through that kind of loss, we have to mourn, and if that includes questioning our reliance on others, even including God, then so be it.

First, Jose had to talk with someone about it. I turned out to be that person because the Catholic Church understands the process of grieving and trains people like me on how to help. Jose and I were able to meet several times in the weeks that followed. He was able to explore all the emotions that had been stirred up as he anticipated a future that looked very bleak to him. I could tell he wasn't used to sharing how he felt, but somehow he got the courage to open up and express his deep hurt.

What seemed to bother Jose most of all was his feeling that God had let him down, that the God he always thought loved him didn't answer his prayers. He wanted to blame God for what had happened; in fact, he was convinced that God was punishing him for not being a better Catholic.

As you can imagine, our sessions together were long and detailed, but very worthwhile. Jose needed to admit that he was a good, loveable person—loved most especially by God. Eventually, he was able to acknowledge that bad things really do happen to good people and that loss was a part of everyone's existence, a natural consequence of our being human and mortal. It was at that point that Jose could begin to move forward and accept that some kind of a new life for him was possible.

Many times when we lose important things, situations, or persons in our life, we experience a deep sense of loss of control. The opposite is also true. Perhaps when things are going well we get the false notion that we are completely in control of our lives. We somehow conclude that we don't have to turn to God for help, that we can manage things ourselves. It is only when things go wrong that we feel God should step in, and if God doesn't do that quickly or completely enough to our satisfaction, we begin to lose our reliance on him.

"I can take care of myself," Gail's teenage daughter, Barbara, said to her. "I don't need your help; I'm not a child anymore."

Barbara was struggling with the aftermath of some biting remarks from her so-called friends. She had told her mother that she was losing her reputation at school because of what the girls were saying about her. Gail, of course, wanted to "fix" what was going on, but Barbara would have none

As long as we live in an imperfect world, there will always be thorns alongside the roses.

of it. Barbara was determined she wouldn't rely on her mother; she was afraid her mom might hurt her as her friends had. She wanted to show the world that she was strong and didn't need anyone fighting her battles. She would rely on herself, and no one else. And yet, the thought of losing her reputation was eating away at her.

Here are a few suggestions that might begin to help all of us as we face the loss of someone or something you hold dear:

- **We simply cannot try to go it alone.** Those who love us (including God) want to be there for us in difficult times. The fact is that a burden isn't half as heavy if there is someone there to carry it with you. (Barbara finally let her mother, Gail, help her think through a strategy that Barbara herself could carry out in dealing with her tormentors. The strategy worked, and Barbara did it herself. But she allowed her mother to help in a way that Barbara felt comfortable.)

- **We have to accept the fact that things will not always go our way.** That is so obvious that it almost goes without say, but it is one of the first steps we need to take in dealing with any grief. There's an old saying: "I never promised you a rose garden…." We must take that saying to heart, even when it is applied to God. As long as we live in an imperfect world, there will always be thorns alongside the roses. We can say, "I want a rose garden with no thorns," but grief itself teaches us that is not possible.

- **We can pray for the help we feel we need.** Maybe we don't know how to pray, maybe we don't really believe in the power of prayer, but we can still pray. Perseverance and acceptance are all part of our relationship with God. Christ gave you an example of this in his prayer of grief in the Garden of Gethsemane the night before he died: "Father, remove this cup from me. But please, not what I want. What do *you* want?" (Luke 22:42).

■ **We must eventually face our grief head-on and begin the difficult work of moving through it.** As I've said throughout this book, it's natural and healthy to grieve what we have lost. Denying it or delaying the process of dealing with our grief will hinder any chance we may have of seeking new life for ourselves. (It was only when Jose finally began to deal with his grief that he was able to go out and find another job that saved his home.)

■ **We have no choice but to accept the fact that loss of any kind—small or large—will change the world we have become accustomed to.** We will be forced to face a new environment, both personal and social. Every ending demands new beginnings. But before that can happen, we have to experience a period of transition. We can use that time to examine what we have lost and what, perhaps, we have gained as a result of the loss we have endured.

■ **We must remember that mourning is a long-term process.** Our grief is unique to us, and so will be the time it takes to work through it. Give grief the time it needs, and it will help you heal.

FIFTH OPPORTUNITY

We will be able to "let go and let God" be in control.

I had the occasion several months ago of working with the parents of a young woman who was going through a divorce. They were well aware of the devastation their daughter was experiencing. And their hearts, as that of all parents do, went out in anguish and love to their child. They spent the first half of our initial meeting trying to explore ways they could help her through her emotional trauma. They even discussed solutions to the financial problems that the divorce was causing her.

The couple admitted they were "fixers" and wanted desperately to mend life and heart of their loved one that had been torn apart. And yet, they couldn't figure out how to be parents to an adult when their only experience had been parenting a child.

So we talked about the need sometimes to let go of what we can't or shouldn't be doing ourselves in order to allow for the maturity that self-growth can bring to others if it is grounded in God. This was so hard for these parents, for they were hurting themselves. They were wounded because of their daughter's wound; broken because of her brokenness.

After a number of sessions, they finally came to the realization that they could still be good parents to their daughter if they simply supported her in small, practical ways as she, herself, tried to get her life together. They had to let go of the "fixing." That didn't mean they would have to stop caring; it just meant that they couldn't do the mending and the healing for their daughter that she had to do for herself.

Certainly the process of letting go is painful. When we are able to hold on to things ourselves, we feel as though we are in complete control. But we know, or should know, that we can't control everything in our life. Some things are just too big for us to handle. It's when we begin to understand this that we can gradually "let go and let God" (as they say in Alcoholics Anonymous). It is the most important and usually the final act of mourning.

When we are mourning a loss, no matter what the loss may be, we may find ourselves holding on to many emotions and feelings that are getting in the way of moving on with our life. Letting go of these emotions—such as anger, frustration, worry, loneliness, sadness, or fear of the unknown—does not mean we are losing control. Giving them over to God is accepting the words of St. Paul: "Live carefree before God; he is most careful with you" (1 Peter 5:7).

 **Letting go of our emotions does not mean we are losing control.**

"I'm afraid if I let go, I'll begin to forget my son," Julie shared with me one day. "How can I be happy again when I know I won't see my little boy ever again?"

Julie had lost her son, Aidan, in a car accident the previous year. Although many people, including her family, friends, and people from her parish, had reached out to her, she refused their help, preferring to be alone in her sorrow and tears. Finally, someone suggested she see a grief counselor, and so with great reluctance, she came to see me. We talked for many hours over a good number of days, but she would always return to the same cry: "I can't let go!"

"What is it you can't let go of?" I asked her.

"I can't let go of the pain," she said. "It seems that is the only connection I have now with Aidan."

"Pain isn't the only connection you have with him," I told her. "The love you shared is the strongest bond you have with your son. It's the pain you need to let go of so that your heart can be filled with the loving memories you have of him. Let the pain go, Julie. Aidan would not want you to hold on to it instead of holding on to your love for him."

"How will I know God is there for me?" you may ask. "How can I find God amid all the noise and chaos that surrounds me? How will God speak to me?"

A young man who lost his wife asked those same questions over and over again. Finally, after much prayer and reflection, he shared the results of his questioning with me in a very thoughtful and poetic way:

> *God knows how much I have grieved*
> *nd how much I have cried.*
> *Subtly, God has taught me that:*
>
> *For every tear I shed, I will laugh.*
>
> *For every sadness I am burdened with,*
> *I will come to know the value of each joy.*
>
> *For every loss I have endured,*
> *I will be further enriched with his peace.*
>
> *For every moment I have doubted his existence,*
> *God will give me an hour, a day,*
>
> *a season to see and feel that he does truly exist.*
>
> *He is there for me and has always been.*
>
> *From the beginning of his time,*
> *spring always follows the winter.*
>
> *After the sorrow of my tears,*
> *there must follow the daffodils of new life.*
>
> *Vincent Marquis, with permission*

Of course we need to work hard at moving through our grief because of nature of the losses we have experienced. But as Catholics we are taught that God will always walk that very difficult journey with us, whether we let him or not. We just need to recognize that God is already there.

Here are some ways we can begin to practice "letting go and letting God" be in control:

- **We can accept the fact that we are human and need help beyond ourselves.** What other choice do we have? Loss can be overwhelming. We clearly don't have all the answers; we couldn't possible have. But there are others—family, friends, professionals—who can help us sort through the questions as we try to sort things out and move on with our life.

- **As counterintuitive as this might be, we can reach out to others who are hurting.** There is a healing process that happens when we open up our heart to others who are in pain. Somehow, our own pain diminishes as we try to comfort the sorrowing. (I witnessed that at a bereavement support group one evening. A young man was telling the story of his mother's death to the group when he began to cry. He managed to stammer, "I can't talk anymore," as he buried his head in his arms. The woman sitting next to him reached out and began to rub his back. After a few minutes, his tears seemed to stop. He raised his head and looked at the group, which had become silent and a bit nervous. With a strong voice, he said to them: "I can talk now. This lady next to me, who I never even met, has given me the strength to finish my story. She reached out to me and shared my sorrow." The woman then said to him: "Comforting you has lessened my sorrow. Thank you for being there for me.")

- **We must be constant in prayer.** We can storm heaven, asking God over and over again for help, and then let God answer our prayers. This help may not be immediately obvious. God's time is not our time; his ways and thoughts are far above ours, as Isaiah says. We have to give God the space to enter our broken heart and mend it. We truly need to "let go and let God."

Heed the words in this lovely little poem:

As children bring their broken toys,
with tears for us to mend,

I brought my broken dreams to God
because he was my friend.

But then, instead of leaving him
in peace to work alone,

I hung around and tried to help,
with ways that were my own.

At last I snatched them back and cried,
"How can you be so slow?"

"My child," he said, "what could I do?
You never did let go!"

- **We can take time to journal.** So many times when we are mourning a loss, we may want to keep all our emotions locked up inside ourselves. We may not want to bother others with our troubles. We may be ashamed and consider ourselves weak. But the bottom line is that if we wish to heal and move on with our life, our feelings and emotions have to be get out in some way. If we can't verbalize them, maybe we can write them down. Journaling can give us an overall picture of ourselves in a very safe way. As we write about what has happened to us, somehow the picture becomes clearer. It's there in front of us, not deeply buried inside us. With the release of words on paper, there can be an easing of tension, for it gives us the opportunity to focus realistically on where we have been and where we are heading. And once we have done that on paper, maybe we can do so in conversation or counseling with others or in prayer with God.

■ **We can make the choice to travel, at least symbolically.** When we suffer a loss, we are given a choice between two roads: one that will help us move forward on our grief journey and another that will leave us standing still. Robert Frost in his poem, "The Road Not Taken," depicts his choice in these words:

> *Two roads diverged in a wood, and I—*
> *I took the one less traveled by.*
> *And that has made all the difference.*

Our grief journey is indeed a road "less traveled," or at least one that we don't choose freely. But if we make a deliberate choice to travel it, it will make all the difference in the world for our healing. One thing we can be certain about: If we have asked God to travel our journey of grief with us, the road has become a little easier to travel. If we have been able to "let go and let God," that road will certainly lead us to a new life and a new world to explore.

AFTERWORD

As you may have already imagined, dear reader, there are many more challenges that await you as you mourn a loss. The thing to remember is that those challenges, if faced and worked through, may yield numerous life-giving opportunities. Look for the challenge; don't hesitate to embrace the struggle that will be necessary to overcome them. It will be through the struggling that you will find many opportunities that can enrich and even bring new life to you.

Try always to remember that you have new experiences ahead of you. You have new worlds to explore and new relationships to grow into. In the process of trying to meet the challenges you are faced with, you can be assured you will find a strength you never thought you possessed. It won't come easily; it probably won't come quickly. But it will come if you continue to work through your grief.

And so:

May the love of God
and the peace of our Lord Jesus Christ
strengthen, bless and console you,
and gently wipe away every tear from your eyes.
Amen.

Mauryeen O'Brien, OP
Hartford, Connecticut

PRAYERS

Morning Prayer

Dear God,

Help me to look for beauty today. May I draw that beauty from every flower and butterfly, from everything that is new and fresh and growing, and from everyone I meet today.

Help me to find your peace and joy in all that surrounds me. May I return that to those I meet today in the form of a smile, a loving word, a kind thought, a prayer, or even a tear.

Help me to find You in all I do and say this day.

Amen.

Mauryeen O'Brien, OP

Evening Prayer

Dear God,

I come to the close of this day and ask you to keep me in quiet and peace. Keep me safe and turn my heart to you that I may be ever mindful of your unbounded love. May that love bless and console me and gently wipe away every tear from my eyes. May my night be a "good night."

Amen.

Mauryeen O'Brien, OP

Prayer When Tired

Father, I come before you today in prayer. I am tired and need to be content with letting your love and understanding wash over me and heal me. Perhaps this is the time to stop and listen to what your sea will teach me. The sea does not reward those who are too anxious or too impatient. Patience is what the sea teaches—patience and faith.

Father, let me be empty and open so I can embrace whatever will be my gift from the sea.

Amen.

Mauryeen O'Brien, OP

Serenity Prayer

God, grant me the serenity
to accept the things I cannot change,
the courage to change the things I can,
and the wisdom to know the difference.

Living one day at a time,
enjoying one moment at a time,
accepting hardship as a pathway to peace,
taking, as Jesus did,
the sinful world as it is,
not as I would have it,
trusting that you will make all things right
if I surrender to your will,
so that I may be reasonably happy in this life
and supremely happy with you forever in the next.

Amen.

A Prayer of Thanksgiving

Father,
I once knelt before you
piece by piece
in dire need to lean on you.
I prayed for you to fix me.
You didn't.
I was still in pieces
so
feeling all alone
I decided to fix myself.

I'm here today
before you,
my pieces all together.
I made myself stand up again.

Thank you, Father,
for giving me what I really needed;
the will at last
to cause myself to heal,
the courage to stand alone,
and the wisdom
to know that I never was.

Vincent Marquis

A Prayer for Blessing

I ask you, O Lord, the Giver of Gifts, to bless me now.
Give me those gifts that I need to continue my journey and
make new choices that will help me to move toward new life.

Amen.

Mauryeen O'Brien, OP

A Prayer to Accept Change

Dear God, an important part of my life is no longer the way
it used to be. Help me to create a newness to my life. Help me
to remember what has been, and to build on those memories
to plan for a new tomorrow. Grant me the courage to face the
dawn of this new life.

Amen.

Mauryeen O'Brien, OP

The Lord's Prayer

Our Father, who art in heaven
hallowed be thy name;
thy kingdom come, thy will be done,
on earth as it is in heaven.
Give us this day our daily bread;
and forgive us our trespasses,
as we forgive those who trespass against us;
and lead us not into temptation,
but deliver us from evil.

Amen.

The Hail Mary

Hail Mary, full of grace, the Lord is with thee;
blessed are thou amongst women,
and blessed is the fruit of thy womb, Jesus.

Holy Mary, mother of God, pray for us sinners,
now and at the hour of our death.

Amen.

The Memorare

Remember, O most gracious Virgin Mary,
that never was it known,
that anyone who fled to your protection,
implored your help, or sought your intercession,
was left unaided.

Inspired by this confidence, I fly to you,
O Virgin of Virgins, my Mother.
To you do I come, before you I stand,
sinful and sorrowful.

O Mother of the Word Incarnate,
despise not my petitions,
but in your mercy hear and answer me.

Amen.

The Prayer of Praise

*Glory be to the Father
    and to the Son,
    and to the Holy Spirit.
As it was in the beginning,
    is now and ever shall be,
    world without end.*

Amen.

OTHER BOOKS ON MOURNING A LOSS
OR DEALING WITH ADVERSITY

Available from booksellers or call 800-397-2282
www.actapublications.com